Jesus loves me, This I Know

the HEALTHKIN FOOD TRAIN

by Jane Belk Moncure
illustrated by Helen Endres

ELGIN, ILLINOIS 60120

Distributed by Childrens Press, 1224 West Van Buren Street,
Chicago, Illinois 60607.

Library of Congress Cataloging in Publication Data

Moncure, Jane Belk.
The Healthkin food train.

Summary: A train carries across the pages dietary
essentials from the different food groups.

1. Nutrition—Juvenile literature. [1. Nutrition]
I. Endres, Helen, ill. II. Title.
TX355.M62 1982 641.1 82-14710
ISBN 0-89565-240-4

1 2 3 4 5 6 7 8 9 10 11 12 R 89 88 87 86 85 84 83 82

the HEALTHKIN FOOD TRAIN

Clickety-clack,
down the track comes
the Healthkin Food Train!

EAT
GOOD
FOOD

Step inside...
take a ride!

BOXCAR
#1
VEGETABLES
and
FRUITS

How corny can you get?
Beets me!
Try these foods every day!
Plum nice!
VEGETABLES

We're the sunshine fruits!
If you carrot all- you'll have us for lunch!
That's the Healthkin way!

and FRUITS

Some are good in pieces.

Some are good served whole.

Some can be
squeezed in a glass . . .

and some served in a bowl.

Just move on down the track.
Car number 2 is waiting for you!

BOXCAR
#2
WHEAT
CRISPIES
CEREAL
OATMEAL
SPAGHETTI
SPAGHETTI
WHOLE
GRAINS,
BREADS,
and
CEREALS

WHOLE GRAINS,

BREADS and CEREALS

Some are good for
BREAKFAST . . .

and some are good for
LUNCH.

Some are good for
DINNER . . .

and here's a crunchy munch!

Y'all come on in!
Step into car number 3.
YUM YOGURT

BOXCAR
#3

DAIRY
FOODS

MILK

COTTAGE CHEESE

DAIRY

Have some dairy foods every day!
YOGURT
Let's butter 'em up!
We are yummy for your tummy!
COTTAGE CHEESE
ICE CREAM

FOODS

Dairy foods
build muscles.

They help your bones
grow stronger.

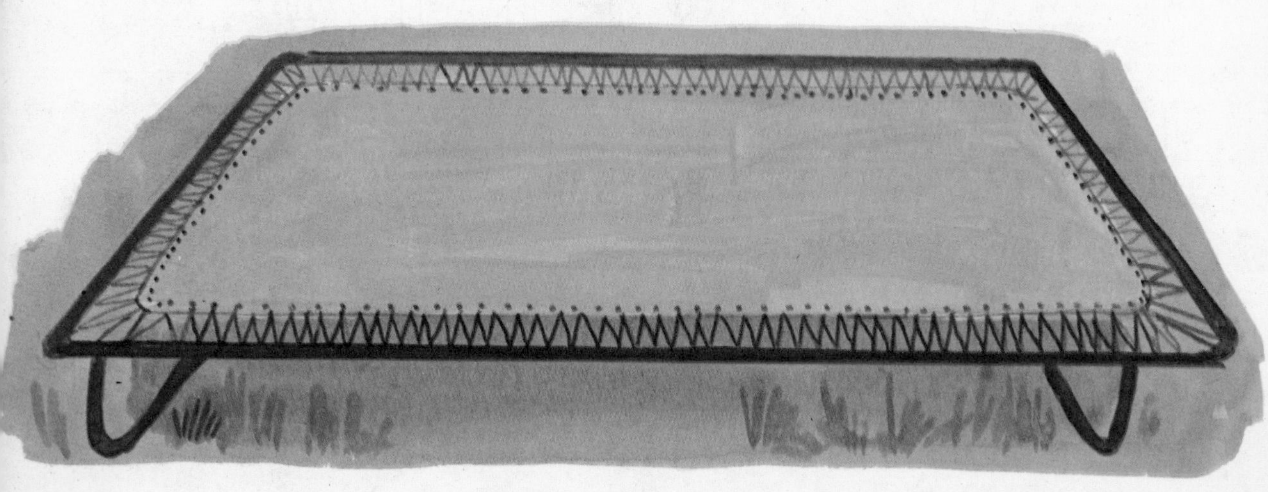

They give you pep
and energy . . .

so you can play much longer!

BOX CAR #4
Try these foods every day!
MEAT

There's egg on my face!
We're nutty
but nice
and nutritious.
That's the Healthkin way!
GROUP

Some are good cold.

Some are good hot!

Some are good in salads . . .

or boiled in a pot!

Oh no! Here comes the
Little Red Caboose.
It's full of . . .

FATS
and
SWEETS

When that Little Red Caboose comes to town, slow down! Try not to eat too many fats and sweets!

Ride the Healthkin Food Train every day
and keep that Little Red Caboose . . .

way back down the track!

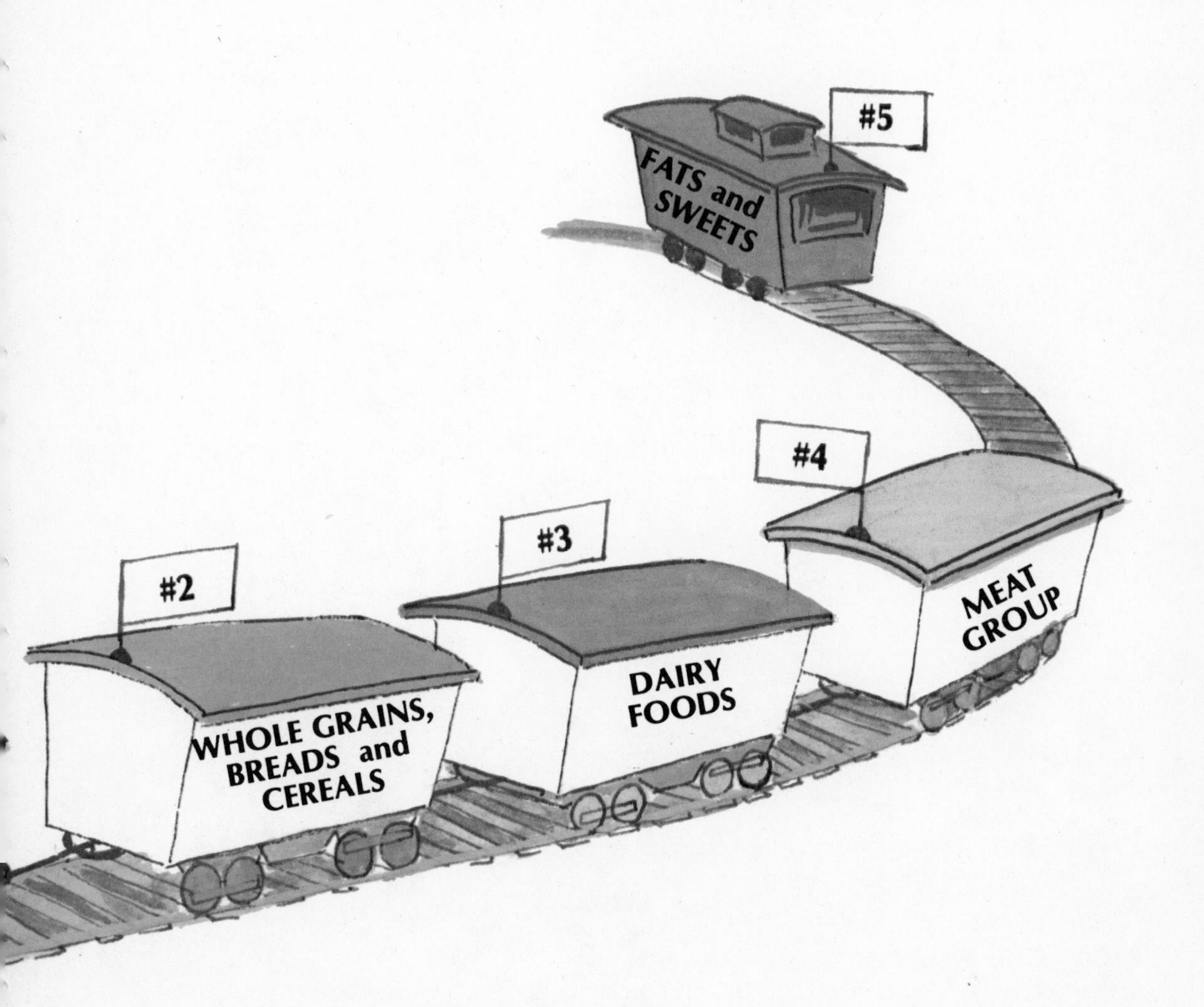